SYAFAKALLAH

MAY ALLAH  HEAL YOU

THE VESPA RIDER

IN THE NAME OF

ALLAH

THE ALL - COMPASSIONATE ALL - MERCIFUL

Other books by The Vespa Rider:

La Taqlaq (Do Not Worry), 2017

Contents

Introduction

I travel with my faithful vespa on random days in solitude, mosque-hopping and observing strangers, capturing moments and discovering life.

Strangers appear in your life as lessons; some as inspirations and others as passer-bys. They impart true wisdom, knowledge and life lessons through their exemplary speech and actions. Then they part ways with you, ending the conversation with the greeting of peace, leaving an indelible mark of appreciation of life in your heart. In those moments we begin to understand life a little better.

"Be in this life as if you are stranger or a wayfarer." - Hadith Sahih Bukhari.

I recently returned from a thirteen month unforgiving isolation or shall I say exile - I was chosen to 'serve' the Singapore Armed Forces in Brunei. Crazy as it is but that was all it took; that was all it took for me to realise that I am done competing, if I only end up becoming what the world wants me to be. I am done trying to fit in, to fake impressions and uniformed, almost robotic expectations of society. I am certain that if I am willing to die for the correct beliefs, I will be sufficed and contented. And certainly in that provision there is true and lasting success and happiness, even when others burden themselves with a reversed impression of me based on humanly created definitions of this world along the way, as it has always been.

Somewhere in those moments reeking blood, sweat and tears in solitude, too many things started to make sense.

True tears are tears for the sake of Allah (Glorified and Exalted be He) alone, and true words that carry depth are often misunderstood and misinterpreted. On this note continues a stream of penned down thoughts of a spiritual journey in my shoes, as a young adult growing and learning to become a true muslim.

In an age where dignity, humility, honour and modesty have become ideals of the past, we the modern generation have become reluctant to ask ourselves of the calamity that has plagued the Earth; we ask ourselves, "Why is this happening?" and if we ask ourselves truthfully, the answer comes back to us in no uncertain terms - we are to blame for this calamity.

I want to change how people see the world, firstly by changing the inward, rather than changing the outward first. I want the world to see peace and love in its purest form again. I have dreams and plans, but Allah (Glorified and Exalted be He) is the best of planners.

I seek guidance from Allah (Glorified and Exalted be He) alone in these baby steps I'm putting forward.

> *"When you have taken a decision, put your trust in Allah." Ali Imran 3:159*

> *"They plan, and Allah plans. And Allah is the best of planners." Ali Imran 3:54*

We subconsciously adapt to how the world works everyday, but we rarely take a step back to attempt to understand what it really means. A loved one once told me, "It is ultimately the effort that He sees, not the amount of knowledge you acquired about a thing. The knowledge will come naturally."

I am 23 years old, and I still lack knowledge about many aspects of Islam. But why should I wait till I have abundant knowledge and numerical 'maturity' to spread simple peace, love and righteousness among people? We tend to expect from people what we ourselves lack giving.

We tend to seek too much of what life has to offer, almost oblivious as to what lies ahead - Death. We tend to live for what is before our eyes, running away from the harsh reality of death. Indeed we will be responsible for all that we do in this life, and every atom's weight of good and bad deeds will be accounted for.

"Verily the death from which you flee will surely meet you, then you will be sent back to (Allah), the All-Knower of the unseen and seen, and He will tell you what you used to do." Al-Jumuah 62:8

"And never think that Allah is unaware of what the wrongdoers do.. He only delays them for a Day when eyes will stare (in horror)." Surah Ibrahim 14:42

Travel and embrace solitude. Look at His signs and creations. Everyday is a lesson. I am what I act. I am what I think. I am what I see. We tend to complain of the plights we are in, without reminding ourselves of our sins. I realized that we are truly what we feed our hearts with. The larger the gap between our principles and our actions only increases the grief in one's heart. Sometimes I sin and found guidance through knowledge. I realized that the knowledge is from the Love and Mercy of Allah (Glorified and Exalted is He) while that sin is from my own ignorance and in naivety succumbing to my lowly desires.

"And whatever strikes you of disaster - it is for what your hands have earned; but He pardons much." Al-Shura 42:30

"I swear by Him in whose hand is my soul, if you were a people who did not commit sin, Allah would take you away and replace you with a people who would sin and then seek Allah's forgiveness so He could forgive them." Hadith Sahih Muslim

Questions of hypocrisy are thrown at self, after each and every single moment I busy myself with contemplation of beauty and materialism. My sins are certain, but will the opposite be accepted I fear. Every littlest of sins kills productivity and darkens the heart. It creates emptiness inside and disowns the heart of serenity and tranquility - the sweetness of iman. It stops the flow of His gift of knowledge. True enough, every shortcomings are from our hands and every blessings are from Him and only Him alone.

"Surely there is in the body a small piece of flesh; if it is good, the whole body is good, and if it is corrupted, the whole body is corrupted, and that is surely the heart." Hadith Sahih Bukhari.

Too often we call ourselves Muslims but we don't really understand what it means to be one. I am saying this for myself first and foremost. We see the unspoken truth of gruesome violence/killings, open fornication, etc to the point where there is no shame in standing up for what destroys/divides us. Modesty and dignity especially; a slow demise. Having said these, if being different brings victory in all aspects and is better for me, then let me be that stranger. When we point a finger at others, there are three fingers pointing back at us. We should change/reform ourselves in order to change/reform the world.

"Islam initiated as something strange, and it would revert to its (old position) of being strange. So good tidings for the stranger." Hadith Sahih Muslim.

If true happiness is what the heart seeks, then let it be known to self that what Allah has forbidden can never bring joy.

"Verily in the remembrance of Allah do hearts find rest." Surah Ar-Rad 13:28

"If you really trust Allah as Allah should be trusted, He would sustain you as He sustains the birds. They go out in the morning hungry and come back to rest in the evening full." Hadith Sahih Tirmidhi

And with this, I end my introduction with a poetry to kickstart the poetic journey that will come after the next few pages.

I've always dreamt of writing my own book
To read, reminisce and question myself
And I'll lay it open on the table, for the ones who'll
take a look
Observing the walking mirrors once they left

And maybe one day too
My child would pick up this same book
And his very own pen
To continue these words,
To reflect,
To humbly amend

If my words could inspire beautifully
The only reason is that my mind is a terrible place
And even if to you these words sound twisted and
silly
The fear of your impression is a burden, and in His
words we find solace.

"Have we not opened your breast (O Muhammad
(Peace be upon him))? And removed from you your
burden, which weighed down your back? And raised
high your fame? So verily, with the hardship, there
is relief. Verily, with the hardship, there is relief. So
when you have finished, then stand up for Allah's
worship. And to your Lord (Alone) turn (all your
intentions and hopes and) your invocations."
Al-Inshirah 94:1-8

Origin

Sinner

Do not get confused

I'm nowhere near a scholar nor a teacher
Nor an influential son of a preacher
But I can't talk about you without blaming me
I guess we're all sinners on different degrees

I just woke up from the anaesthesia sleep
And they are already giving me dozes of morphine
I'm losing sight, I am losing grip
But I wanna write to remember, recognizing the
pain within

We are who we are till we make it this far
But have we ever questioned how did we end up
this way
We are living through a pain for that beautiful scar
And you think the glamorous fools will get away

We all have a share of His Signs for the kind and
the cold
He makes available His Mercy to each of His mould
To ensure we fulfil our purpose and play our role
So seek your own sincere journey and not leave it
untold.

"Wondrous is the affair of the believer for there is good for him in every matter and this is not the case with anyone except the believer. If he is happy, then he thanks Allah and thus there is good for him, and if he is harmed, then he shows patience and thus there is good for him."

Hadith Sahih Muslim

Fearless Silence

Do not take silence as a weakness
For maybe he is busy fighting with his self
And do not take words as arrogance
For he could be reminding himself

You may have a gain
That you may lose tomorrow
In a form of a pain
That will cure your sorrow

It is both a calamity and a blessing
To look at everything so deeply
It is both tiring as it is healing
But lives are meant to be led ever so fearlessly.

*"But as for him who feared standing before his Lord,
and restrained himself from impure evil desires, and
lusts. Verily, Paradise will be his abode."
An-Naziat 79:40-41*

Ink

I am not here to please
And I seek no attention
What I earned only Him will ease
And in His Words I seek protection

I take pride in the ink that I lay
Being one of the ways I escape
It has never bothered much the rhyme I portray
But the message it brings for remembrance sake

In the decisions that I'll make
In the roads that I'll take
Even when everything's at stake
Let it not be fake

So let not your tongues hurt yourself
For the way you choose to want it read
Let not your heart ruin your mental health
Hatred is not born but certainly bred.

*"Read! In the Name of your Lord, who has created
(all that exists)" Al-Alaq 96:1*

Human

I'm only human
I err and I yearn

Handsome is the man who lowers his gaze
Humble is the man who sujood and prays
Wise is the man who limits his words
Calm is the man who supplicates

Through experiences, He gave thoughts and
wisdom
I thrive and I fail, in this very freedom
With every sin, on qalb is a drop of blackness
Hence fill me with fear, for I will be weighed in
absolute fairness

What I am, is a sign of where I am heading
I seek Your remembrance, hoping wellness in all
paths I'm leading
I write and write, till there is nothing left
For these words are reminders from self to self.

*"Verily, Allah does not look at your appearance
or wealth, but rather He looks at your hearts and
actions." Hadith Sahih Bukhari*

Turning Heart

Torn between love and separations
Pushed and pulled into violence and clean actions
Driven and disappointed between failures and
aspirations
It disgusts me to be a happily confused creation

So I grew up observing people and questioning
what this life brings
And I developed my own hypothesis believing it
would heal
But something once so close could turn into a
distant longing
So ask the turning heart about the empty soul - what
do you feel?

The wisdom didn't come from the books you read
But to contemplate the understanding of words you
meet
Understanding is in vain if it lacks visualization
But the visualization is never enough without
internalization

So what good is contemplation
What good is contemplation if it's deprived of
action
I guess it is arrogance
A worse form of ignorance

Hiding what he earns till it fades away
Remind me to give away hoping it will stay -

Wisdom.

"O you who believe! Answer Allah (by obeying Him) and (His) Messenger when he (may peace and blessings be upon him) calls you to that which will give you life, and know that Allah comes in between a person and his heart. And verily to Him you shall (all) be gathered." Al-Anfal 8:24

Path

I've slept and breathed with the ruthlessness of
gangs
And sat and listened to the knowledge of the pious
Never have I witnessed hardships to those lengths
But where we end up is where the heart desires

I've been outcast, exiled, to learn with the maestro
of the jungles
And made friends with the child of the soulless rich
Walked and talked with the wealthiest homeless
Never selecting where He place, and how He teach

I take whatever life gives me
But what does that make me?
I can only learn from what I see
And we'll become what we'll be

So don't mistake me for my calm, careless
disposition
That makes you just another judgemental fool
Don't take pride in your comfortable position
Each and every being is born in a different school.

*"It is better to sit alone than in company with the
bad; and it is better still to sit with the good than
alone. It is better to speak to a seeker of knowledge
than to remain silent; but silence is better than idle
words." Hadith Sahih Bukhari*

Grave

I stare at the ground
I clenched this very soil
With the grief that surrounds
Into deep thoughts I toy

To whom we impress
Are they worth the pain
To whom we oppress
For that loss we gain

We fill this cup with facades
Drinking it up thinking it'll suffice
All these while it's been lies to ourselves
Are we blinded or have we no sense

We settle for so little compared
Unimaginably lesser to what He has prepared
Ignoring the Signs we learned
Only to be punished for that grief we earned

O Allah, nobody understands this unrest
Who I was, what I've been through and how I give
my best
I seek calmness, applying sense with what you give
For those who mock what others have received.

"Beautified for those who disbelieve is the life of this world, and they ridicule those who believe. But those who fear Allah are above them on the Day of Resurrection. And Allah gives provision to whom He wills without account."

Al-Baqarah 2:212

Selfish

I know that the second that passed
Is either for me or against me
Sometimes we hide behind our own masks
We say they are oppressed but are we truly free?

Because too often we seek what ourselves don't
give
Too often we blame others for how we live

Remembering the grief of my wasted time
How much do I have to pay back to the world for
all those crime

So keep yourself in sajdah
And let no one see your tears
So you fight for what is right
Even if nobody hears.

*"Indeed, Allah will not change the condition of a
people until they change what is in themselves."
Ar-Ra'd 13:11*

What if

What if I knew the time of my death?
What would I do with the time I have left?
What if my sins are written on my forehead for the
world to see
Knowing people judge and how ashamed I would
be

What if each day I'm revealed the punishment for
each sin
Who then would I blame for where I've been
Questions arise in this spot I sit
I hear the azan, tears fell, I got lost in it.

*"And if Allah had willed, He could have made you
(of) one religion, but He causes to stray whom He
wills and guides whom He wills. And you will surely
be questioned about what you used to do."*
An-Nahl 16:93

Death

From You we come
To You we return
The questions alarm
Turn by turn

Imagine the sight
The anxious plight
Will there be light
Deep down inside

As I lay out my hands and lower my gaze
As You lower my body, will You widen my grave?

When all is said and done, what is left?
Don't these thoughts matter to you and me?
It fills the void I created myself
It kills the pain what others don't see.

"And if you could see when the angels take away the souls of those who disbelieve (at death), they smite their faces and their backs, (saying): "Taste the punishment of the blazing Fire." Al-Anfal 8:50

Journey

Questions

These words I wrote for myself
Are these same words that I present to you
They are reminders firstly for nobody but myself
Of which I hope may benefit every one of you

For reminders benefit people
The people who fear the One who created you and
me
Now let's make this simple
I'll ask you a few questions, though you're not
obliged to answer me

What if tomorrow won't arrive?
How would you spend your today, being fit and
alive
Or what if we die while on a very shameful sin?
Are we prepared to be resurrected on where we've
been?
Allah swt gave you and me Islam but what are we
doing with that blessing
Allah swt gave you and me Islam, but what is the
meaning of being a muslim.

*"I swear by the Day of Resurrection and I swear by
the reproaching soul (to the certainty of resurrection).
Does man think that We will not assemble his
bones?"Al-Qiyamah 75:1-3*

Nature

I observed the swaying trees
Under the bright full moon
I enjoyed the cool night breeze
It is close to midnight soon

I covered the moon as I raised my thumb
And then I tried to pinch it too
How could these beauties be overlooked making us all numb
What blurred our vision and veiled this view

Where came the mountains?
Where came the detailed vast species?
Days and nights never fail in turns
And we dare walk with pride in this land of His

Even in our own selves are Signs, will we not then see
We are pretty much nothing, yet we are everything but free.

"And on the earth are signs for those who have Faith with certainty, and also in your own selves. Will you not then see?" Adh-Dhariyat 51:20-21

Arrogance

I looked up to the sky and I admired the birds
How they kept silent and roamed elegantly in those
heights
And then I observed people who speak but lost
meaning to their words
How depressed and oppressed they are in that
image and in that facades

How their words wasn't reflected in actions
Hope and fear that corrupt the most innocent of
hearts

I grew tired of talking so I decided to observe
And noticed too many people smirking
Arms folded with two feet up their desks
How can there be arrogance if it is love that you
deserve?
The fact is you're depressed
so you oppress
no one but yourself.

*"So proceed through the earth and observe how was
the end of the deniers." An-Nahl 16:36*

Bystanders

You see the path of truth
How so little are following it
So beware the path of falsehood
How so many are destroyed by it

Do not be discouraged by the first
And do not be deceived by the latter
Yearn for something true more than the quench of a
thirst
Don't grow old with regrets not doing the simplest
things that matter

I guess this world is a dangerous place not because
of evil
But because of the bystanders looking at it
That is a greater shame, a greater evil
Being sane yet doing nothing about it

Has the sin become so routine
That repentance becomes unnecessary
Has the sin become too routine
That we let it pass, till The Day arrives - the
punishment hefty

Maybe our souls are not evil to begin with
I'd prefer to say we have grown remorseless

I have a turning heart wanting to be filled, pretty
much empty to begin with
I'm a searching soul that motivates a body that was
once useless

So guide me, and not leave me astray
So remind me, will you must if you may?

Remembrance

The oppressed
The orphans
The unfortunate loved ones
Randomly appear in my head
"Do I deserve this comfort if they are still in
melancholy?" I said

Sometimes we put ourselves into so much grief
Forgetting that there greater ones seeking relief
Tonight, for you I write, what I prayed, that I hoped
for in myself
May Allah remember me too and help me during
my death

"Righteousness is not that you turn your faces toward the east or the west (in prayers), but (true) righteousness is (in) one who believes in Allah, the Last Day, the angels, the Book, and the prophets and gives wealth, in spite of love for it, to relatives, orphans, the needy, the traveler, those who ask (for help), and for freeing slaves; (and who) establishes prayer and gives zakah; (those who) fulfill their promise when they promise; and (those who) are patient in poverty and hardship and during battle. Those are the ones who have been true, and it is those who are the righteous." Al-Baqarah 2:177

Hypocrite

I fear the day knowledge comes with ease
And I'll speak what I don't practice
I fear the day my lips move
But my mind wanders
When I prostrate to the One I love
But soul wanders
I fear the day I hold back what I could give
I fear the day I become a hypocrite
I fear it most when I don't even realize I am it
I fear it most
When I don't even realize I am it

What we spilled has evaporated
Not something we pick up from what is scattered
May our speech now only be for wisdom
For that self-restrain is a mark of freedom.

*"And when they meet those who believe, they say:
"We believe" but when they are alone with their
Shayatin (devils – polytheists, hypocrites, etc),
they say: "Truly, we are with you; verily we were
but mocking. Allah mocks at them and gives them
increase in their wrong-doings to wander blindly."
Al-Baqarah 2:14-15*

Empty Cans

It takes pain to recognize a blessing
It takes mirrors to find self in another
It takes sincere words to fill what is missing
It takes a lot to start over

But at times we have so much to say to the world
As much as we give so much of ourselves to it
Till we become empty cans in the words we hurl
Finding faults in another man's heartbeat.

*"Indeed, Allah will not change the condition of a
people until they change what is in themselves."
Ar-Ra'd 13:11*

Self-Delusion

His Deen is perfect
For our well-being, filling up what we lacked
We seek, He gives and we forget
Is it ignorance or are we just, scared

Scared of what people might say
As if they put the food on our trays
"You never cared less, and now you wanna pray?"
Say, "Stay if you wish, but not lead me astray"

I guess oppressions ultimately by self to self
Feeding the feeling of lacking -
There is no end,
There is no wealth

Taking comfort and provisions for granted
Retaliating in every form of distress
Complaining of what is fated
As if we are in charge, and we know what's best

I write this note for self before the rest
Surely those pleasures and hardships are truly just
tests.

*"And when We bestow favour upon the disbeliever,
he turns away and distances himself, and when evil
touches him, he is ever despairing." Al-Isra' 17:83*

Rise

We are ourselves when we are alone
Yet we are not born in a world that way
A world made of a million stones
The hearts of many men till the Final Day

But this heart and mind

It is not meant to stoop so low, but for a higher
purpose
Redefine definitions to seek a bigger find
For a complete book you need a verse
Why focus on an atom with an endless mind

We build all these analogies in our heads
To walk on this earth ever so lightly
For we are born with different fates
But why are we walking so uniformly

Ever so blindly, so forgive me
For the style and my way of my learning
I may come off to you as ever so passive, so
uncreative
But through my silence I am doing the gaining.

*"So have they not traveled through the earth and
have hearts by which to reason and ears by which to
hear? For indeed, it is not eyes that are blinded, but
blinded are the hearts which are within the breasts."*
Al-Hajj 22:46

Betrayal

Desires made slaves out of kings
As much as patience made kings out of slaves
But some things shouldn't keep us waiting
Many have brought their dreams of change to the
graves

The sins made were like fire
Possibly burning deeds like wood
We err and we give in to the worldly desires
I asked will my soul reach its throat the way it
should

Each time repentance is delayed
The return will just get harder
It is our own soul we betray
As the gap grows wider

So He blinds us to 'enjoy' our suffering
Or suffer in our own 'enjoyment'
He leaves us with everything in nothing
And He gives nothing but what for us was written.

*"Their example is like someone who lights a fire, and
when it lights up his surroundings, Allah takes their
light away and leaves them in darkness unable to
see. Deaf, dumb and blind - so they cannot return."
Al-Baqarah 2:17-18*

Belief

You do not live to be liked
By people who hate themselves
Nor do you live to hate
The people who are so full of themselves

But you travel these lands and those seas
To observe the consequences of their actions
Know that many influences are either lessons or a
disease
Unknowingly settling you into useless directions

I say these too much with a different rhyme
Because belief without reminders wears through
time.

*"Our Lord, let not our hearts deviate after You have
guided us and grant us from Yourself mercy. Indeed,
You are the Bestower." Ali Imran 3:8*

Innocence

We're supposed to pick ourselves up from failure
Chasing what they say about success
But how about what it truly means
From the eyes of a child
Innocent
Unoppressed

Or from the tongues of the wise
Where you derive hidden gems in their speech
Know that they too come from Allah, The Most
Wise
They are sent by Him, the One we beseech

And then observe the speech of the fools
Where they think they live only by their efforts
Use their judgements like tools
And embrace the good in their words

Be patient
Overcome as it comes
Actions are by intentions
We are our only harm.

*"And whoever is blinded from remembrance of the
Most Merciful - We appoint for him a devil, and he
is to him a companion. And indeed, the devils avert
them from the way (of guidance) while they think that
they are (rightly) guided." Az-Zukhruf 43:36-37*

Naive

Many times people are taken in by the
arrangements of words
Instead of the deep subtle message engraved in it
Many times people only see the surface of the
world
But avoids the roots of it all, that leads up to it

Every minute a soul is enlightened
While another man grieves
How the first earned what he yearned
While the grieving man knows, but hates to
believe

So question your spirituality in the midst of all
physicality
In the eyes of the weak and the mighty, putting
them in parity

And there is no better source to speak and start
upon
Other than the ones you seek from yourself
It is from your plights that lessons are drawn
To revive the dying heart and the mental health

Where were you and what did you do
That justifies the strength He loaned to you
And why now the complaints and tantrums you
threw
He tries whom He loves, if only you knew

A man who acts upon true knowledge has no fear of
this world
He has control of his desires and the shield
to what they hurl
I guess we are all striving for that, from the natural
within
It is just that we grow to obtain it through
different means.

Hearts of Men

Everybody can imagine, exaggerate or lie
But none can speak in full truth of what the limbs
didn't do
So we'll say anybody can try
But none can fulfil the potential of a heart that's true

So what makes you
What makes your heart you
From everything you've been through
But a general point of view
From a reflecting mind and heart that
renews
Intentions, remembrance, anything but
without a clue

Many a times people attempt to heal
While avoiding to embrace or share the pain
We forget the essence of knowledge that we
unknowingly kill
While the disease of men blindly remain

I'll keep writing endlessly without
exhausting the lungs
Believing that one day the hearts of men will
overshadow the voices of its tongues.

*"So which of the favours of your Lord would you
deny?" Ar-Rahman 55:13*

A Collection

Everyday I arrange my observances into rhymes
Unknowingly causing them to fill me
Playing it over a million of times
Becoming the man in the words that I see

I realised that we are all a collection
Of the inner voices, the emotional distractions
The words that we read that resulted in actions
And the everyday images we see becomes our
created assumptions

So we accumulate all these memories
To create a path of our 'own'
A plan, a map, an idea or a list
The highs and lows in each unique tones

Just be careful what you swallow with age
Don't make it the cause of your very own prison
Don't let others hold the pen to your page
And say you're the cause of your own poison.

"That Day, We will seal over their mouths, and their hands will speak to Us, and their feet will testify about what they used to earn." Yasin 36:65

Beautiful Irony

It's a beautiful irony

How He suffices and restricts for a term
How He grants struggles as a way to learn
How some are seen worthless yet are the richest
How the famous are idolized yet are the loneliest

Take lessons beyond your own circle
And bring it into reflection in your solitude
Then observe how humility can result in miracles
So seek forgiveness when you see changes in
multitude

Make it the journey that you bring with age
Into a book that will close when you reach your
grave
Reopened on The Day where it will all be weighed
Not missing an atom from the actions we made.

*"When the victory of Allah has come and the
conquest, and you see the people entering into the
religion of Allah in multitudes, then exalt (Him) with
praise of your Lord and ask forgiveness of Him.
Indeed, He is ever Accepting of repentance."*
An-Nasr 110:1-3

Self-Blaming Tears

For all You gave and all You've taken away
I pray once again to not let this heart astray
The Signs are clear, the promise is true
Yet our hearts go blind, true ones are few

Be a man against anger and desire
Islam's a remedy like water to fire
Be ashamed and cover each sin
For He is One that is Most-Forgiving

Struggles brought me wisdom every each day
The same way pleasures could take it all away
In hardship and solitude was I close to You
I'd rather stay in that state of calmness, than be
'happy' being far away from You

We create these sins from our very own hands
But truly the best of those is the one who repents
Self-blaming tears as I write this note to self
That the condition of my surrounding – a reflection
of myself

And I still write and write till there is nothing left
To remind myself of what I had and what I'll have.

"It is the same (to Him) concerning you whether one conceals (his) speech or one publicizes it and whether one is hidden by night or conspicuous (among others) by day. For each one are successive (angels) before and behind him who protect him by the decree of Allah. Indeed, Allah will not change the condition of a people until they change what is in them selves. And when Allah intends for a people ill, there is no repelling it and there is not for them besides Him any patron."

Ar-Ra'd 13:10-11

Your House

God be my witness
For the written reflections in Your house
God be my witness
For how I seek true life in those towns

That this is my story
And my form of glory
An invitation to Your Beauty
An antidote to my worry

I ask of You to guide me
Please suffice me
Protect me
In this very journey.

"Travel through the earth and observe what was the end of the deniers." Al An'am 6:11

Night Prayers

Don't you ever write from that
influenced mind
For you'll never find words that can
move your soul
Seek the curves by that ink through that
repenting heart
And you'll see yourself pouring from
your natural mould

Don't you ever judge this world from
only those eyes
For you will be painfully blinded by the
worldly lies
For it's the state of the heart that
unveiled the facades
How the world celebrates killing the
purest of hearts

I have seen intellectual men grieve and
wanting to tear
But instead suppresses himself into deep
torture
And then I see a man with everything
but a worldly fear
Who cries at night only to walk this
world with deep pleasure.

"Is one who is obedient to Allah, prostrating himself or standing (in prayer) during the hours of the night, fearing the Hereafter and hoping for the Mercy of his Lord (like one who disbelieves)? Say: "Are those who know equal to those who know not?" It is only men of understanding who will remember (i.e. get a lesson from Allah's Signs and Verses)."

Az-Zumar 39:9

The Silent Cries

He cried in his prayers
He cried for us in his prayers

He cried for the orphans today feeling
alone
He cried for our families now war-torn
He cried for the widows feeling grief
He cried for our sick ones seeking relief

And I told myself
Shouldn't I cry for the poor I did not feed
Or for the salah I did not meet
Shouldn't I cry for the ill words that I
spoke
And for those hearts I once broke

I know I'll cry for the time I lost that will not return
And I'll cry for His words I did not learn
Maybe I'll cry too for the preparation I did not
make
Cry for the punishment that I may face
What deeds to the last breathe will I actually take
What am I really, but just a couple of days.

*"Two eyes will not be touched by the fire, an eye that
cried from the fear of Allah, and an eye that stayed
awake guarding for the sake of Allah."*
Hadith Tirmidhi

The Night

I felt the need to write
As I observed the sensitivity to how nature moves
Before the flashing thoughts come out of sight
I'll give myself in to what sooths

I could almost grasp it so clearly
Everything moved so slowly
So gracefully
Such quiet uniformity

A gentle night breeze
With soft subtle rain
Trickled down my skin, nothing felt
amiss
Nothing felt bleak, nothing felt in vain

The hall felt spacious
As the hurt became painless
As I read Your Words through the pages
There was a beautiful scent, in this heart
a war of emotion wages

A thousand months, even better
See the measure He gives - thoughts that
linger
Allah if last night was The Night
Grant me light upon light

For I feel I haven't done enough
For this is my plea
For this is my plight

I ask of You O Allah to fill me where I lack
To forgive all my faults
To grant the good I seek
To suffice what I plead
To accept all my deeds
And to teach what I need

Don't take the *ajr* of this month away from me
Don't take the best thing that has ever happened to
me

If these flowing cooling tears, are words being coy
May I humbly write to remember, this night of
quiet joy.

"Indeed, We sent the Qur'an down during the Night of Decree. And what can make you know what is the Night of Decree? The Night of Decree is better than a thousand months. The angels and the Spirit descend therein by permission of their Lord for every matter. Peace it is until the emergence of dawn."
Al-Qadr 97:1-5

The Month

I must be dreaming
For it has gone way too fast
The times we spent together
Will soon be in my book of past

One day we may all forget
The coming and going of this month
And so I lay here
Into deep thoughts I stare
Trying to tell this and that to You
How much I really do care

What I learnt about time
Is that it eventually runs out
So I won't say goodbye
But I'll see you soon instead
And if the day would come
Where our paths would meet
I would want to say to Him
That I will try again.

"Indeed We have revealed it (Qur'an) in the night of Power. And what will explain to you what the night of Power is? The night of Power is better than a thousand months. Therein descends the Angels and the Spirit (Jibreel) by Allah's permission, on every errand: (they say) "Peace" (continuously) till the rise of Morning!" Al-Qadr 97:1-5

Love

The Book

In Your name
I craft this form of speech
As a remembrance
Of Your Perfect Words I beseech

You have made The Book a guide
From You to your creation
But you see them burn the light
Don't they realize it's a futile action

Allah make my looking and listening
A form of worship
Let The Book be my love
Let it sink so deep

Make my reciting
A deep pondering
Then let me recite what I pondered
So it stays a lesson, a hope I can bring

Do not seal my ears
Or curtain my sight
Let it cancel my fears
Grant my heart calmness and that form
of light
Do not make me heedless
Or recitation a waste

Be gentle on me, have mercy on me
Guide me on this world
These tests
In most beautiful of ways.

"(This is) a blessed Book which we have revealed to you, (O Muhammad), that they might reflect upon its verses and that those of understanding would be reminded." Sad 38:29

"And We have certainly made the Quran easy for remembrance, so is there any who will remember?" Al-Qamar 54:17

The Call

What is it about the call and the prayers
That brought these beautiful tears
What about it
That cancelled all these fears

What is it about the prostration
That stopped the time
This feeling
This ease
A state so sublime

Understand your fears
Love the ones you hold dear
Get on your way
Wipe off those tears
Know that they'll not always be here.

"Worship Allah and associate nothing with Him, and to parents do good, and to relatives, orphans, the needy, the near neighbor, the neighbor farther away, the companion at your side, the traveler, and those whom your right hands possess. Indeed Allah does not like those who are self-deluding and boastful."
An-Nisa 4:36

The Source

Allah swt is Al-Wadud, The Ever-Loving
Love that heals, as we cause our own
bleeding
I asked for what you deserve, as if they are
mine
And I distanced my presence, so I won't
cover your shine

Just why should I love you more than Him
If He is the One that made me known to you
Why should I ask of you for that love within
If He is the Creator, of that heart in you

For I fear betrayal
If I attach myself on what's not mine
But I keep you in my prayers
In case you'll be making it fine.

"Love your beloved moderately, perhaps he becomes hated to you someday. And hate whom you hate moderately, perhaps he becomes your beloved someday." Hadith At-Tirmidhi

Through You

I observe and I wonder
As He made you known to me
Your exemplary actions made this heart
unknowingly grow fonder
So this is how a true Muslim should be

Through you He planted seeds of guidance in me
Putting me into this path of light and knowledge
May He blow away your sins for that faith you see
For maybe through you I was pulled off
the edge

Breathing Islam and knowing you is a dream
That character in you, that rarity, one of few
So why should I love you more than Him
If He is the One that made me known to you

If this distance is what I should endure
Let me hug you with my duas, in them my feelings
pour
May your love for Him be true and pure
Hence being in Jannah with you I intend
to secure
And to the other forms of Signs

I have yet to meet you
The one out of the few

I have yet to meet you
But I know you are true
I have yet to meet you
But I know I have You

Allah.

"And in the creation of yourselves and what He disperses of moving creatures are signs for people who are certain (in faith)." Al-Jathiyah 45:4

Move Along

The world in its nature is in perfect order
But we tend to complicate what is simple
I'm reminding myself that isn't perfect either
That you will be betrayed with regards to
people

Betrayed by your own attachment that you
allowed yourself to be dependent on
We all meet for a reason
A need
To learn
And to move on.

*"O mankind, you are those in need of Allah, while
Allah is the Free of need, the Praiseworthy."
Fatir 35:15*

Nights Like These

Nights like these
They are supposed to mean something
To please those who seek, to say the least
In the memories I cling, in the moments I miss

But to love is to prove
To feel is to approve
In the hearts you move
Through His Decree He sooths

Now I am facing tomorrows I can't get hold of
While holding the hands of today
I'm seeking to ask for yours in which I
know not of
Hoping to create a better one,
Some day.

"And hold firmly to the rope of Allah all together and do not become divided. And remember the favor of Allah upon you – when you were enemies and He brought your hearts together and you became, by His favor, brothers. And you were on the edge of a pit of the Fire, and He saved you from it. Thus does Allah make clear to you His verses that you may be guided." Ali Imran 3:103

Maybe

We lost the meaning of voice
What more the meaning of words
Like how many lost the meaning of love
Settling for what lurks

Maybe words are meant to uplift
Maybe words are meant to teach
To teach you how to breathe
How to live
Yet could deceive
If we aren't what we preach

Maybe love require acceptance
Maybe love is to calm the heart that turns
To teach that what could cure
Or may be your only medicine
Can become something so impure
A self-oppresion in our own poison

So words aren't really from a creative mind
But just another sinner who observes
Himself before others, to remind and to refine
To return to its fitrah, to the heart that deserves.

"There are two statements that are light for the tongue to remember, heavy in the Scales and are dear to the Merciful: `Subhan-Allahi wa bihamdihi, Subhan-Allahil- Azim (Glory be to Allah and His is the praise, (and) Allah, the Greatest is free from imperfection)'."

Hadith Bukhari and Muslim

Hold My Hand

Fascinate with your mind
Speak through your signs
Love as though you're blind
Trust me, we'll be fine

Remind me that these dangers are real, yet
fear is a choice
Just another product to the thoughts that I
create
Hold my hand, walk on this earth with
compassion and poise
And travel these lands, learn through
observance of the humans' fate

Dear, the world is corrupt, and we're taking sides
Healthy, wealthy yet unhappy, so what is it
we're taking pride?

*"So have they not traveled through the earth and
have hearts by which to reason and ears by which to
hear? For indeed, it is not eyes that are blinded, but
blinded are the hearts which are within the breasts."
Al-Hajj 22:46*

Blank Photographs

We capture photographs of the beauty of its form
And then let it pass as though it was nothing
We go back, and we conform to the norm
If everything had a purpose, aren't they
telling us something?

The alternations of night and day
The reason for the breeze and the heat
Down to the the tiny drop and a line of ray
If we are powerless, then who's behind it?

Now walk the earth with questions and
compassion
Compare the mindless obeying nature and
the 'educated' humans
How one fashions life in a form of
oppression
And how the other still provide despite our demons

Remind me to not be of those, with hearts
that are blind
That made their eyes useless, a cause of
their plight.

*"Indeed, in the creation of the heavens and the earth
and the alternation of the night and the day are signs
for those of understanding." Ali Imran 3:190*

Cheap

If only people knew how to love for His sake
Would this world end up in this sorry state?

Humans are to be loved
And things meant to be used
To opposite of above principles we serve
Morals, chastity and chivalry is what we lose

The world is everything it shouldn't be
Cheapen and lowering our souls to a certain degree
From trending lustful fashion
To 'love' in a facade of lusty attraction

I speak not excluding myself
For I too err and once fell into those traps
But I write to remind and to correct myself
So will you remind me too, perhaps?

If only people knew how to love for His sake
Would the world still end up in this sorry state?

To the ones who truly see
And to the ones who learn
May the One for whom you have loved another
Loves you in return.

"Beautified for people is the love of that which they desire – of women and children, heaped-up sums of gold and silver, fine branded horses, and cattle and tilled land. That is the enjoyment of worldly life, but Allah has with Him the best return."

Ali Imran 3:14

Strangers

I tiptoe through these lands
Without a clear view where it would lead me
Through a journey of words, I'll make amends
Why hold a man down from wanting to
be free

Cos you will never understand what you
have
Until you intentionally or unintentionally lose it
The reason I crossed seas and travelled
through lands
To appreciate what I had in the land
where I bleed

You'll meet people just like you
In similarly different skins
Who loved unconditionally
Through very different means

Hear them out
Give them your time
He'll clear your doubts
In a different rhyme.

*"Say: "Travel in the land and see how (Allah)
originated creation, and then Allah will bring
forth (resurrect) the creation of the Hereafter
(i.e. resurrection after death). Verily, Allah is
Able to do all things.""*

Al-Ankaboot 29:20

Define Love

Dear Allah as I looked above
Just what is it that they define as love

Will she have the patience of Asiyah
Or a heart filled with bashfulness, or haya'
Will she have the purity of Maryam
Being protectors of one another from
every little harm
Clad her with a tad of Aisyah's sincerity
Let these heart fall upon these values,
these varying beauties

But we humans seek what we ourselves don't give
Hence I tell this soul to seek in her, equal to how it
lives
Make us strangers and wayfarers of this earth
Brought together for a higher purpose, for The One
we serve.

Dear Allah as I looked above
Just what is it that they define as love.

*"Corrupt women are for corrupt men, and corrupt
men are for corrupt women. Good women are for
good men, and good men are for good women."*
An-Nur 24:26

Have Faith

I yearn for what I don't deserve, possibly
To miss so much what I've yet to see
Living a quiet dream, holding on to a silent promise
O Allah, strengthen my iman in these queer unease

A heart that differs from majority
By God-fearing and reticent piety
What I seek I believe is true beauty
Firm wisdoms and gentle haya', such a
beautiful rarity

Talk is cheap unless it's truly words
from the heart
If it's meant to be, truth is, nothing has
ever kept us apart

But as for now I want to guard my heart,
body and soul
To understand the meaning of life as a whole
In Allah's remembrance there is no loss
The Pen has lifted, it's my name by yours

May Allah protect you and your loved ones
May Allah continue to strengthen your
akhlak and your iman
May Allah further increase you in knowledge and
wiseness
May Allah shower you with beautified
characters in abundance

You're always in my thoughts and in my
prayers
We'll cross paths one day wonderful stranger
Because if soul mates are written, and
meant to be
I place my heart solely in Your hands,
guard this soul that'll be the one for me.

*"And of His Signs is that He created for you from
yourselves mates that you may find tranquility in
them; and He has placed between you affection and
mercy. Indeed in that are Signs for a people who give
thought." Ar-Rum 30:21*

Too Much

May Allah swt help us for we are
surrounded with too much 'beauty'
That we're deceived into ignorance of the
cruel world out there
Man how can we have eyes and limbs yet
still seek pity
Friend how can you have so much and still
say this life is unfair

Or maybe it is

In our hoarded wealth our good health and
not feel guilty
In all our fake competitions of who is worthy
When there are disabled orphans crying out there
with tattered clothes all dirty
When you show all your skin and they beg
for clothes just to feel 'pretty'.

"Indeed mankind, to his Lord, is ungrateful."
Al-Adiyat 100:6

One Day

One day someone will come by
And see meaning behind your words
She will understand the wisdom behind
your speech
And appreciate your actions
She hears the thoughts behind your
silence
And share that love behind those tears

And she will marry those thoughts
She'll be a companion to your speech
She will partner your actions
And be one with the beautiful silence
She'll embrace the love behind those tears
She'll hold to the hands of your shared visions
And walk with you in your travels

She will come by
And complete you

Allah swt knows best.

God-Willing

You and I
God willing, you and I will meet again
When we're least expecting of it
One day in some far off of a place
I will recognize your face
We'll reminisce the days
We'll praise Allah
For His Wisdom and Grace

But for now
I'll slowly drift away
In solitude I play
In solitude I pray
In the solitude of days
I'll make something of what I say

Let me live this quiet dream, holding tight to a quiet promise
I ask of Allah, strengthen my Iman and cure this disease

"...And when you have decided, then rely upon Allah. Indeed, Allah loves those who rely (upon Him). If Allah should aid you, no one can overcome you; but if He should forsake you, who is there that can aid you after Him? And upon Allah let the believers rely." Ali Imran 3:159-160

Signs

I tried to quieten my thoughts to hear the
recitations clear
How He gave Signs through the words that I hear
Something that's been missing He brought it so near
How something so simple yet made it so dear

I stayed, I laid on the praying mat
Thinking what if one of our time was near
What good were the memories we had
If we die in a state of err

I stayed, I laid on the praying mat
Thinking if I could meet my death here
With it my pain was shared
In these tears lies my love and fear

*"Woe to every sinful liar. Who hears the verses of
Allah recited to him, then persists arrogantly as if he
had not heard them. So give him tidings of a painful
punishment." Al-Jathiyah 45:7-8*

Letters From Exile

The Birds

I am losing track of days
While chasing after time
What is with all your noise and craze
Judging my silence as a crime

Tonight
I manifest my thoughts into words
For those that laugh as others hurt
Don't they look up the sky and observe the birds?
How they fly by days and come back fuelled

How they first took the plunge
And came back stronger than ever
How others took a punch
And came back wiser than ever

We tend to chase after things we deem as
success
Till we lose our very own selves in the slow process

So what is it that you really want in your
life?
And for whom you do it for?
Are they worth your strive?
Were they the ones who healed your sore

Everybody is fighting, so you fight hard
And know that among creations you stand alone
And our days are numbered right from the very start
Till He puts it all to a stop, and we'll die alone

Think about your thoughts
Wasn't it Him who guides
And all the strength you got
Hadn't it all been Him who provides

We are nothing but our own mockery
To think we are our own guarantee
We are nothing but our own mockery
To think we are our own guarantee

I write and write till there is nothing left
For these are reminders from self to self.

Forgive

Melancholies aren't necessarily defined by
tears
Neither do laughters cancel all fears
The one void of tears may just be arrogant
And the one with overflowing joy could just be
illusioned
I tried to close up our distance with prayers
And I found contentment in that focused
gaze

The presence of wisdom in every test
Demonstrating patience and gratitude in
what is less
May we be granted firmness and pardoning in times
we are oppressed
May He forgive us in those times we
knowing and unknowingly transgress

From family to acquaintances
To the moments in between
I left them all to take my chances
I would like to come back strong,
And I would like to come back clean.

"Say (on my behalf), "O servants of Mine who have acted recklessly against their ownselves, do not despair of Allah's mercy. Surely, Allah will forgive all sins. Surely, He is the One who is the Most-Forgiving, the Very-Merciful." Az-Zumar 39:53

Be

Be silent
Be silent until the world understands that the
absence of noise is indeed beautiful
Because the smarter you get the lesser you speak
Because before true knowledge is wisdom and
observance, you are what you seek

Be a voice for the voiceless
By falling in love with silent expressions
Look at contentment like a quench of a thirst
Do not be shaken
Be that man of vision
And be the woman with ambition

Be angry, but not bitter
To prove no one but yourself, you're fitter
A fighter
Who can love better
Channelling that fire into positivity
That you can be everything they're not, and that a
tough man don't require pity

The right to freedom of speech consists of nothing
but truth
And that's where I usually stand, even alone, yet
unmoved
The world in its nature, is in perfect order, but we
tend to complicate what is simple

I'm reminding myself that you will be betrayed
with regards to people

Betrayed by your own attachment that you allowed
yourself to be dependent on
We all meet for a reason, a need, so that we'll learn,
and/to move on

If my words could inspire beautifully
The only reason is that my mind is a terrible place
And even if to you these words sounds twisted and
silly
The fear of your impression is a burden, and in His
words we find solace.

Tripped

I'm withholding my anger
Though I'd like to be the strangler
Of the box in the neck where the voice comes from
The one that stirs this burning storm
It's not my right for him to insist
That he acknowledges my existence
But time and time again he displayed a complete
lack of respect
As if he' s the very source of my sustenance

So he coops himself up in his room
And start imagining things
He's actually just manically depressed
To rehearse that fakeness to impress
To earn the praises of the rest
Fearing his sustenance behind that very desk

It' s destroying him slowly- the fake yet demanding
world
It just whirls him in a frenzy, as he twists and he
twirls
Spirals and spins till he hurls himself into rage
Trying to pry himself out of his shrinking cage

So he tries to push and pull me
But he knows that he can't fool me so he's mad
He has no choice but to scream and raise his voice
up at me
Cause it annoys him to see that I ain't one bit scared

So he just tortures himself
With his fortune and wealth
Extorting people's happiness to get his dough
Thinking I would stoop low to his flow

Don't we realise that our body is a trust, and it will
return to Him
He led many astray, and kept them blind
My world isn't what it seems
But neither is yours, a solution we live to find

The world is not meant for us to survive in it
But for us to last till a better Day where everything
would fit
We'll be raised for what we see and what we did
The reason why we are still fighting, till death
arrives and that's it
That's it

I keep observing
And I'll wonder and I'll reflect
I'll keep writing
The rights of Allah, people and myself I'm learning
to protect.

Gratitude

Too often we say what we don't mean
Too often we fail to ponder what we see
I chased after happiness as if it could be seen
But it is gratitude that's been absent in me

I asked for a path of my own
And this is the path You gave
Hence this is the path I chose
Hence this is the path I crave

From family to acquaintances
To the moments in between
I left them all to take my chances
Maybe I could come back strong
Maybe I could come back clean

Because the angel of death does not discriminate
What have we done to peacefully accept our fate
Maybe we should be deprived to appreciate
May these steps, these words, substantiate

Because if this is Islam, I want in;
Again and again.

"Indeed, those you worship besides Allah do not possess for you (the power of) provision. So seek from Allah provision and worship Him and be grateful to Him. To Him you will be returned. And if you (people) deny (the message) - already nations before you have denied. And there is not upon the Messenger except (the duty of) clear notification. Have they not considered how Allah begins creation and then repeats it? Indeed that, for Allah, is easy. Say, (O Muhammad), "Travel through the land and observe how He began creation. Then Allah will produce the final creation. Indeed Allah, over all things, is competent.""

Al-Ankabut 29:17-20

You Are

You are the people you meet
The conversations you share
The films you watch
The rhymes you listen to
The lines and curves of your words from your pen
Those are the dreams you seek

You are a collection
With a unique mind
So drown yourself in your existence
Let all of the fire run through your veins

To the feet that only fits your shoes
To the mouth that only speaks for your downfall
and your good
To the rough skin that makes up your shield
Make known to yourself what you feel

So I ask of you to clench your fist but keep it down
Softening your heart in a way that toughens you up.

"O you who have believed, respond to Allah and to the Messenger when he calls you to that which gives you life. And know that Allah intervenes between a man and his heart and that to Him you will be gathered." Al-Anfal 8:24

I Wonder

They ask me am I okay,
And they ask me if I'm happy
Are they asking me that
Because of the trials that's been thrown at me
Or are they asking me that
Because they don't see what I see

Do they genuinely care
About all this pain that I bear
Do they genuinely care
When its been me here and you there

So you talk about me, him and her
Like you can see through what's in here
So you speak as if you have no fear
From a heart that is unsound and unclear

If only their eyes saw souls
How ugly would we be
If we were born with permanent blindfolds
How would the term 'love' then be seen

So be terrifyingly strange
Or in a way silently beautiful
And observe how our fates were arranged
For the ignorant and the ones mindful.

Purpose

I am not here to please
And I seek no attention
But I see a world deeply diseased
In His words I seek protection

Maybe we have been cut too many times that we
forgot how to feel
That it has become 'me, myself and I' that we
forgot how to heal
Because we abandon the Quran
Because we abandon istighfar and zikir

So don't talk if you don't have substance
But those who have substance don't talk
So where does that sits me?
This life has made me solid but emotionless as a
rock

What is it about your strength that makes you strong
When you drown yourself yet you try to breathe in
a world you don't belong
People don't see the path you took, people don't
care about the path you'll take
Time and time again He made you realise that
you're on your own, unless you do it for His sake

So be respectful enough for your own good
But be firm enough not to let self be stepped upon
I've taken this much from this world and this is my
loot
And I realise The Day will come where this is what
I will be raised upon.

*"Do men think that they will be left alone on saying,
we believe, and not be tried?" Al Ankaboot 29:2*

Window Panes

I looked out the window panes
I quieten my thoughts despite the landing planes
I filled my ears with your Perfect Words
Shutting out all the factors that could hurt

I pondered over Your creations
Reflecting on my very own actions
May I see this world from a different view
Different from those who turn away from what is
true

I know that the second that passed
Is either for me or against me
Sometimes we hide behind our own masks
We say they are oppressed but are we truly free?

Because too often we seek what ourselves don't
give
Too often we blame others for how we live

As I remember the grief of my wasted time
How much do I have to pay back to the world for
all those crime
How much I want to heal others with the purpose of
healing mine
How badly I would like to make it all fine

I realised that whatever I have today
Was never mine to begin with
They are nothing more than to distract
Nothing more than to deceive

I know that I have to start with myself
I know that I don't have much time left
Am I wrong to think I can change the world
And man up to the words that they hurl

So keep yourself in sajdah
And let no one see your tears
So you fight for what is right
Even if nobody hears.

"And if you should count the favours of Allah, you could not enumerate them. Indeed, Allah is Forgiving and Merciful." An-Nahl 16:18

In Solitary

I looked up to the sky and I admired the birds
How they kept silent and roam elegantly in those
heights
And then I observed people who speak but lost
meaning to their words
How depressed and oppressed they are in that
image and in that facades

I used them as mirrors
A reflection of my errs and my flaws
How I am part of the ummah but didn't justify these
tears
So I write, hoping to remember hoping to open
some doors

I claimed my rights but forgot my duties
I yearn for success but still fear sacrifice
So here I am, thousands of miles from home a
million more from comfort
In solitary I'm learning to appreciate the blessings
in our ties

Has a Sign not come and we denied
You see none of us are denied guidance, but we
only chose to ignore
Isn't that arrogance, an intentional ignorance
Till death reaches the throat while we gaze on

I saw, I felt and I fear
But still I slip and I err

So help me, pull me up when I fall
Don't judge me, but forgive me for all my flaws.

*"Say, "If Allah had willed, I would not have recited it
to you, nor would He have made it known to you, for
I had remained among you a lifetime before it. Then
will you not reason? So who is more unjust than he
who invents a lie about Allah or denies His signs?
Indeed, the criminals will not succeed."
Yunus 10:16-17*

Refuge

La tahzan, innallaha ma'ana
He sent words from above the seven heavens telling
us not to be sad
We are as we see Him, however near, however far
So I asked myself as I woke up breathing, how am I
this depressed?

I've been long here and a long way from home
Writing these words, among His creations I stand
alone
Trying to remind myself that the whispers are
imminent, but your grief is a choice
What is sadness and anxiety, inability and laziness,
but the devils' toys

So you ask with heart, and you ponder over it
That with Allah is better recompense than any type
of loss
If your heart is with Allah, then why are you
grieving over it?
He delays only due to reason and wisdom, He
promised a way, He'll open some doors

O Allah I seek refuge in You
From anxiety and sadness
I seek refuge in You
From inability and laziness

And I seek refuge in You
From being overpowered by men and this sense of
loneliness

Allah swt will ease our trials and afflictions and
raise our ranks
But will we or have we ever stayed true, or even
ever gave thanks?

*"Secret counsels (conspiracies) is only from Satan
that he may grieve those who have believed, but he
will not harm them at all except by permission of
Allah. And upon Allah let the believers rely."*
Al-Mujadila 58:10

The Fire Within

I started from nothing, but now i'm hard as a brick
I'm smiling to their emptiness, as they strut down
big
They're just opening up their weakness, and I feel
no kick
Cos i'm sick of those same tricks tryna make their
own life click

I play our videos and continuously stare at pictures
of you
I never got to say I love you but please know that I
do
Yeah I say it now, and you can't hear me
So what good does that do
So I let it be
I let it be and keep the emotions true

They say grievance has a way of affecting everyone
different
Man how can you touch so many lives and just
leave me here hanging
I still hold to your cloth your smell and love how its
made of cotton
The time, the rage, the tears, the voices builds up,
that leaves me either violent or fallen

Cause sometimes you just feel tired and you feel
weak
And when you feel weak, you just wanna give up
But you gotta search what's within you and try to
find that inner strength
To be everything they are not, use that spark to get
psyched back up

And sometimes I just lay on the praying mat
Having shut the windows and locked the door
I stand and I kneel, and I prostrate and I sit
Admitting my fears and my every single flaw

I kept videos of peoples' pain
And I listened to their plights and their voices
How much have they lost and how much have I
gained
I know I'm stuck, but why should I give in to be
trained
To have no brain
That forgotten fact drives me insane

Composure and contentment descends
How much I love the oppressed strangers, the wise
and quiet friends
And how much sometimes I hate myself, for
wasting time giving in to what bends
I ask of Allah to give me just enough fire, to give
warmth to the one who fans.

Grey Clouds

Grey clouds walk in line
As the nights came, the days died
But still I live to tell you mine
Still I wake up to the morning light

We tend to live for someone we love
'To him I give', 'to her I share'
How long more, till we leave this Earth
Till we realize, did they ever really care?

I've got a different approach
To dealing with emotions
People will leave you, kindly or in the lurch
Ask yourself is it worth - all these worldly
devotions

I look up to all your strengths
Hiding that hurt to all pretence
Tonight I relate to the stories you share
Avidly listening, to the ground I stare

And when I'll finally see you smile all day
Let go of my hand, I want gone
I'll pray, with two hands I lay
When I see you heal, I won't stay on.

"Love the one whom you love to a certain degree (moderately), perhaps one day he will be someone for whom you have hatred, and hate the one for whom you have hatred to a certain degree (moderately), perhaps one day he will be one whom you love."

Hadith At-Tirmidhi

Boatman

They say the tongue of the wise is behind the
heart
While the heart of the fool is behind the tongue
And with these few words, do allow me to start
As I picked up lessons, from another man's junk

I carry all these loads
Across seemingly impossible roads
I felt my bones collapse and my mind explode
Forced to wake up strong in that very same boat

Now I can barely prostrate
The position that allowed me to escape
How the world was made for you, mister
While you were made only for the Hereafter
A million of 'what ifs' would never have sufficed
You took that road, and now you'll pay the price.

Mission

I'm on a mission to decipher how I should lead my
life
On the other hand on a stage where I should bring
my life
I've returned to having what I need within my
reach, but why do I miss the times where I needed
to strive
Should I lead?
Or should I follow?
Am I firm as steel, am I solid?
Or I'll just bend to what leads cos I'm hollow?

I learnt to hate or adopt identities that I observed
As I listened to the mistakes the success and the
roads that I conquered

I've been bullied and I've been the bully
I've been taken in, stripped, whacked, interrogated
for something too silly
I've seen blood on my hands as a result of my rage
I've been outcast and exiled for a year, a time
served to grow doubly in age

I've been trying on different masks according to the
circles I am in
To fit and blend in, to see where I belong, where I
can bare what's within

These are parts of my share in this world, all
temporary
But at times I hold on so much to it as if it's eternal
Someday my prayers and my actions will be my last
It's just your deeds and words for others that stays
when you leave this world

So I record it, much to peoples' judgement
Though I'll not rest on your hate to become my
burden
Seen so much like you so often so common,
wasting time giving in to what bends
So I ask of Allah to give me just enough fire, to give
warmth to the ones who fan.

*"And remind, for indeed, the reminder benefits the
believers. And I did not create the jinn and mankind
except to worship Me. I do not want from them any
provision, nor do I want them to feed Me. Indeed,
it is Allah who is the (continual) Provider, the firm
possessor of strength." Adh-Dhariyat 51:55-58*

No Desire

I am in no desire to compete
If you become what they ask for
I am in no desire to fit
Squeezing myself into that door

I've my own anomalous dreams that I seek
The written thoughts that I brainstormed
In a world that only augments what's bleak
A dedication to the art of my form

I am tired of what's mundane
Words without soul, being dumb yet sane
I am tired of loving and living without intellect
Saying, that's just how it goes, what do you expect?

So you join the system
Taking pride in hoarding wealth for a term
You adjust and you squirm, till you slowly sink in
shit
That 'happiness' you lied to yourself, you'll slowly
die in it

Me?

Again I'll be going away
In solitude I play
In solitude I pray
In the solitude of days
Hoping to come back to you in the best of ways.

Poison

Wash the poison of those people off my skin
And show me how to be real again
Till you allow them to enter this heart within
They will just be dust that sticks, or very small
little stains

The knife was literally at the side of my head
What do you think I was going to do
Go on, slice me down to pieces I said
I fear only God, do you really think I was going
to fear you too?

At times the heart tries to make the head its fool
There's a thin line between fear and anger, leave
one in the heart, the latter at eyes
So let them observe, and you'll walk away
And let them understand the wisdom behind
your lies

When you're willing to die for your belief
Then no one can manipulate you
That is weight off the shoulders, much like a
sign of relief
When you know the rights of Allah, yourself and
the many other few

God sets us on a path always for a better reason
And the holes that you fall into, are not by questions
of permission
So when your journey is done, you can only hope
that you'll do good
And you'll get on your way, knowing that you did
what you could

You'll know when it is over, so admit when it is at
its end
You come forward, and shake life's hands like a
man
And maybe my child will pick this same book and
his very own pen
And continue these words, to reflect, and to humbly
amend

Now what bothers me the most
Is to pick up where I left off
I'm free from a place where all time froze
Now how do I break these walls down soft.

Our Share

He's on a mission to decipher how he should lead
his life
On the other hand on the stage of where he should
bring his life

The knife was literally on the side of his head
What do you think he was gonna do
Go on, slice me down to pieces, he said
I fear God, do you really think I was gonna fear you
too?

He's been bullied and he's been the bully
He's been taken in, stripped, whacked, and
interrogated for something too silly
He's seen blood on his hands as a result of his rage
He's been exiled for a year, a time served to grow
doubly in age

These are some parts of his share in this world, all
too temporary
But at times he holds on to it as if it's eternal
Someday your deeds and your prayers shall be your
last
Will it ever be enough to peacefully leave this world

If all his words could inspire beautifully
The reason is that his mind is a terrible place

And even if to you it sounds twisted and silly
The fear of your impression is a burden, and in His
words we find solace

If you're willing to die for your belief
Towards you no one can manipulate or deceive
They'll slowly understand, they'll slowly perceive
The wisdom in what you held back, or allow to
receive.

Exile

It's coming to a year
And I'm still here
It's already a year
And I'm still here

When you're exiled
With only yourself as a helping hand
You fight to survive
Till your legs give out
And it's still not the end

What is fear?
When the end line - home is unclear
Till you mentally give your home up
And tell yourself
This is my plate
This is my cup

Know that God is your only constant
How much can we really go through in order to
learn?
But who am I to say that I am better, or learned than
you
Till I fear God and only God, in the way I handle
you

Even till my brains blow up and my bones collapse
I'll still pick myself up, because choices makes you
weak, perhaps

Cause the tongue speaks of its heart at its death
And this is what I've gained, after the days I have
left.

*"Get used to a rough life, for luxury does not last
forever." Umar Ibn Al-Khattab*

Tiba-Tiba Jiwang

Tidak semestinya erti menangis itu sedih
Dan tidak semestinya yang ketawa itu bahagia
Manusia yang tidak menangis langsung itu
sombong
Manusia yang terlalu bahagia itu lupa
Aku mengubat rindu dengan du'a awal ke hujung
Kiniku mengerti kebahagiaan itu apa

Hadir hikmah dalam cubaan
Mengajarkanku kesabaran
Menghayati erti kesyukuran
Maka untuk mereka sebaik-baiknya balasan

Sayang dan rindu antara keluarga dilafaz
Melalui kalimah Allah yang dihafaz
Dirasai dalam hati
Lain tidak memahami
Bukankah ini hadiah Allah kepada kami
Bekalan untuk yang lebih indah dan hakiki

Indahnya Islam seisinya
Apabila menyayangi keranaNya

Semoga airmata rindu menjadi alasan kami
mendapat Syurga bersama
Sampaikan salamku ya Allah, kepada yang ku cinta
Iaitu keluarga.

"But you prefer the worldly life, while the Hereafter is better and more enduring."

Al-A'la 87:16-17

Aftermath

It's all coming to an end, its all coming to a close
This is the life, a life I've been caged upon
So when I'm free, why does it feel like this was the
life I chose
The only thing I know the most, a world I was
meant to be raised upon

I can't seem to fit to the free man's accord
Unless I unlearn everything my brain was taught
Do I really belong to this kind of world, I thought
I layed my hands, I looked up, in Him I sought

It's not that I'm ungrateful or showing disrespect
To the years before this that I was raised upon
But we are men with a mind and a healthy intellect
But when we have comfort, why are we blinded
from the hearts that are torn

How many times should I say this with a different
rhyme
I guess cause we are human, and we need reminders
for your heart and mine.

Repercussions

I asked for a path of my own
And this is the path You gave
Hence this is the path I chose
Hence this is the path I crave

From family to acquaintances
To the moments in between
I still remember the moment I left them all to take
my chances
Hoping to come back strong, hoping to come back
clean

Thirteen months later

I came back with so much wounds that I forgot how
to feel
From the unpublicized land of 'me, myself or die'
that I forgot how to heal

Don't speak if you don't have substance
But people who have substance don't talk
So where does all those episodes sit me
A life that released me solid, but emotionless as a
rock

The journeys that passed
Is now either for me or against me

Sometimes we hide behind our own masks
We say they are oppressed but are we truly free

Its the fifth month since homecoming
Yet I am still coming to terms with the inner
conflicts
The social conditioning and the spiritual longing
The current physical limitations now too with the
pain it brings

I know that nobody is having it easy
And taking it easy makes us weak
So let my own flaws and faults keep me busy
From the judgements of men and the 'substance'
they speak

I asked for a path of my own
And this is the path You gave
Hence this is the path I chose
Hence this is the path I crave.

Society

Calamities

Don't you see calamities on a large scale
Meant to test on individual levels
I keep asking how will I pass in the moments I
fail
In the evil of His slaves and the taunts of the
devils

Too many words are made out for the broken
heart
As much actions are taught to piece them back
together
Everybody may know, but what sets you apart?
To piece up not only the broken, but all that
shatters

Not all that lived, survived to see
And not all that sees, are able to hold to that
vision
It is how much we want to be free
Truly free from this inner oppression

*"Our Lord, let not our hearts deviate after You
have guided us and grant us from Yourself mercy.
Indeed, You are the Bestower." Ali Imran 3:8*

Dreams

Women raped and killed for being Muslim
Man shot in the midst of takbir, a martyr, a muazzin
Children are slowly burnt
While our brothers buried alive
Others are waiting for their turn
Hoping for a reason to survive

Know that these things are happening
But nobody speaks without a worldly gain
We turn away from the help they are seeking
How can we be dumb and deaf yet purely sane

And nobody actually cares
For righteousness suddenly nobody dares
Shutting their ears to what is outside their comfort
zone
Leaving them oppressed and all alone

But when That Day arrives
And for sure it will
Indeed the patient will thrive
And you will hope their wounds would heal

He provides none of those strength
For you to misuse to this length

So tonight

My silence will be silenced
And I will speak
It is not the noise
But the righteousness I seek

It hurts and it's not going away
We all feel your pain
Even when it does
The scars shall remain

The agony of love
I have for you
Requires our presence you deserve
Your dreams will come true

Patience
I ask of you.

"And what is (the matter) with you that you fight not in the cause of Allah and (for) the oppressed among men, women, and children who say, "Our Lord, take us out of this city of oppressive people and appoint for us from Yourself a protector and appoint for us from Yourself a helper?" An-Nisa 4:75

Inner Oppression

Are our hearts really beating?
For our silence is a crime
Indeed mankind is at loss as we are only watching
Allah swt swore it by time

So ask yourselves is it okay?
Is it okay as long as it doesn't happen to you?
What is this life but just amusement and play
We're just gonna live and die and not be questioned
too?

This world, this dunya is not for you and me
We are oppressed yet they say that we are free
Know that one Day we'll be questioned for all these
pain that we see
Have we no heart nor sense to just let them be?

*"Never will you attain the good (reward) until you
spend (in the way of Allah) from that which you love.
And whatever you spend - indeed, Allah is Knowing
of it." Ali Imran 3:92*

*"Go forth, whether light or heavy, and strive with
your wealth and your lives in the cause of Allah. That
is better for you, if you only knew." At-Tawbah 9:41*

The Signs

It has been quite a while since I sat and lifted up my
pen
The moment it's laid on paper I remembered the
unfortunate souls
The best of the sinners are the ones who repent
So won't we come back before the lands crumple
for Truth to unfold

When can we ever cry over the state of the ummah
If I allow myself to be angered over this mess
How can we ever escape the manipulation of the
kuffar
When I can't keep steadfast the Deen for the good
of self

How can we not fear as we see each of every Signs
Of The Final Hour coming alive right under our
noses
This mess is built by the 'knowledgeable' minds
Fueled by the ignorant and the immatured losers

So which one are we
And where sits me
Question what you see
The world is what you'll be.

"Do they then await (anything) other than the Hour, that it should come upon them suddenly? But some of its portents (indications and signs) have already come, and when it (actually) is on them, how can they benefit then by their reminder?"

Muhammad 47:18

Deaf, Dumb, Blind

The thing is
We have grown arrogant, believing that tomorrow
would come
We say we are young
It is all calm
There is no harm

So we fill our lives with senseless music
With purposeless romance
With the poisoning fame
And immoral trends
In those facades we seek amends
And we feel as though the world is in our very
hands

We yearn for things we think could fill this growing
void
So we blindly mirror what society thought
We turn to them thinking we'll heal this very heart
Will they be your help in that hole, in that
graveyard?

We yearn for the blessings we see in others
But we forget the trials that come with it
And don't despise your trial and all the others
For surely there are blessings in it

For all He gave and all that He has taken away
We ask Allah to not let this heart astray
We created all those sins from our very own hands
But truly the best of those, is the one who repents

May Allah swt guide our actions
He is All-Seeing, He is All-Aware
For He is the Most Sufficient
The Great Disposer of affairs.

Definitions

Happiness.
Define that.
Loneliness.
Is it sad?

Different.
Is it odd?
Success.
In the papermoney we hoard?

In you is it passion in vision
Or just another peer oppression

For we are lied into the definitions that others create
And worse influencing another into our materialistic
beliefs
Till you see babies grow into whom they imitate
Becoming uniform robots that loves what deceives.

*"When it is said to them: "Follow what Allah has
sent down." They say: "Nay! We shall follow what
we found our fathers following." Even though their
fathers did not understand anything nor were they
guided? And the example of those who disbelieve is
like that of one who shouts at what hears nothing but
calls and cries cattle or sheep - deaf, dumb and blind,
so they do not understand." Al-Baqarah 2:170-171*

Nightly Questions

What if your purpose differs from what you're
taught to believe
What if the destruction we receive comes in a joy
that deceives
What if your happiness doesn't lie in the popular
ideas that's conceived
What if I say that you have the freedom to shift

What if I say that a success story could lie in the
gift to breathe
And that all the wealth you 'earned' was just a
useless myth
Would you have held back what you could possibly
give
Or when you made it to the one or three, would you
have fought for the fifth

These are just nightly questions that I accompany
myself with
As I fall asleep hoping not to drift
Hoping to wake up not in a state of filth
But with fire in his heart, an idea up the sleeve

"O you who believe! Stand out firmly for justice, as witnesses to Allah, even though it be against yourselves, or your parents, or your kin, be he rich or poor, Allah is a Better Protector to both (than you). So follow not the lusts (of your hearts), lest you may avoid justice, and if you distort your witness or refuse to give it, verily, Allah is Ever Well-Acquainted with what you do."

An-Nisa 4:135

Fake

It's my right to insist on how much my soul actually
needs
And then comes society - false expectations and
fake impressions
Offering with the left, saying whatever feeds
So we become empty shells - float where the water
leads

You were once free, now you're saying you're
making ends meet
And then they'll wash their hands off you
"That is the path you yourself chose to walk
indeed."
"I never forced you, I'm just a soul that's untrue."

Our fear of the impression of another made us
helpless
So help yourself
For His sake
May you be firm
May you be fearless.

*"And if you obey most of those upon the earth,
they will mislead you from the way of Allah. They
follow not except assumption, and they are not but
falsifying." Al-An'am 6:116*

He Knows

May Allah swt grant wisdom and success
May His Words sooths and caress
To those who remind and remember death
To those, who could have

Speaked but be selectively silent
Fought but walked away
Blindly enjoined but observes to learn
Regretted the last but maximised today

He recognizes your struggles
And He promised you good
For that war from all angles
The firmness in your belief, and the reliance you
put.

"You will surely be tested in your possessions and in yourselves. And you will surely hear from those who were given the Scripture before you and from those who associate others with Allah much abuse. But if you are patient and fear Allah - indeed, that is of the matters (worthy) of determination." Ali Imran 3:186

Closing supplications:

"O Allah (Glorified and Exalted be He) You are Pure from all defects and all praise belongs to You Alone. We testify that there is none worthy of worship but You. We seek Your pardon, O Allah (Glorified and Exalted be He) and turn to You in repentance.

May Allah (Glorified and Exalted be He) bestow His choicest blessings and mercy on the best of His creation Muhammad (may peace and blessings be upon him), as well as on his family, his Companions, his wives and all his progeny."

Lastly, I seek no personal credit but to remember me in your pious du'as for whatever benefits you may have derived from this book.

Fee Aman Allah.

INTERVIEW ARTICLE

Meet The Vespa Rider: Inspirational Author Of "Syafakallah", Traveller & Poet

featured on
www.havehalalwilltravel.com
by Sharifah Nawwarah

https://www.havehalalwilltravel.com/meet-the-vespa-rider-inspirational-author-of-syafakallah-traveller-poet

Poetry on faith, from self-discoveries to documenting soulful writings - this is what the author of Syafakallah, May Allah SWT Heal You and La Taqlaq, Do Not Worry shares about in his books. Going by his pen-name, The Vespa Rider, he shares with us what inspired him to write these things! Read on to find out more.

1. Tell us a bit about yourself!

A struggling soul who seeks to observe life to its details while remembering the certainty of death in the uncertainty of time; what have I done to fulfil the rights of the Creator (Glorified and Exalted be He), the Prophet (may peace and blessings be upon him), my family, self and others to be able to meet death with a safe smile, God-Willing. I am no different from any other man, and we all are born to lead inspiring lives in our own ways. I only chose to speak to others bits and pieces about mine, documenting memories, hoping someone after myself would take heed.

2. How did you come up with your pen-name 'The Vespa Rider'?

Through the calmness and tranquility that I realised a mosque can fill this soul, it moved my heart to go mosque-hopping with my ever-faithful Vespa. The antique Vespa by itself teaches and reminds me the values of gratitude and humility in some way or another. Furthermore, it holds a deep sentimental value due to its service for me in my own personal journey of 'hijrah', being the most vital mean in my journey of solitude. If you'd ask for one worldly and material thing that I love, my Vespa would be the answer without any doubt, for how it has actually assisted me in my travels towards Allah.

When my book was launched I realised that I needed a pen-name to uphold my choice of being anonymous as much as I can, due to various reasons. So The Vespa Rider it is, till today alhamdulillah.

3. What inspired you to write 'Syafakallah'?
Every single one of the reasons why I wrote Syafakallah were summarized by the verse in the Quran explained by Allah (Glorified and Exalted be He) and sayings of Nabi Muhammad (peace and blessings be upon Him).

> *"Indeed, Allah will not change the condition of a people until they change what is in themselves."*
> *Ar-Ra'd 13:11*

> *"Remember more often the destroyer of pleasures - death." Hadith Tirmidhi*

"When a man dies, his good deeds come to an end except three: ongoing charity, beneficial knowledge and a righteous son who will pray for him." Hadith Muslim

Do you see the flow and relation of these three verses? I have always been a man who observes, wonders and questions why the world and all that is within acts the way it does down to its minute details; accepting and rejecting opinions and certain practices in my head through the observations I made. And at the end of the day I realised that the world can never be changed until I change what is within me. Every minute death draws closer and what have I done or accomplished to meet it with a safe smile.

Another reason is that I wanted something physical for my future children or generations to look through, learn from, and improve on, or the least, to understand the life of one of their ancestors briefly. Not to leave a legacy or to be recognized by many, but more of a beneficial reminder for self and another.

4. Do you have any advice for writers who'd like to write a book on poetry or travelling?
Write for all the beneficial unseen values you wish to build

within yourselves, before it is meant to benefit another, which explains the second point - never write to please another creation but write only to please the Creator. Ask yourself having written every word, would the Creator approve this? Write in a state of gratitude and humility, and it can never be derived without sincere worship. Aside worship, give with sincerity, for example be it ten cents or ten minutes for a homeless man, and you'll be given abundantly. Who knows, one of the endless increase of sustenance by Allah might just come in a form of wisdom in writing.

Travel for the right reasons and know that every moment or observation holds a deep lesson to be told, so hold a notebook and a pen everywhere you go. Let not the scribbling and mistakes end for editing can be done later but inspirations are often easily forgotten.

Lastly, be discreet in your 'success', to stay away from the naysayers that could diminish your fire or the praisers who could bring about arrogance in this weak heart of ours.

5. Describe your ideal writing environment!
The note-taking of observances and moments could come from anywhere and anytime, but I usually piece my words

together while I am in a mosque at night. Most of my final editing and reflections will then be done on my bed before I go to sleep or when everyone else is asleep. Moments of solitude usually craves for an enlightened mind.

6. In your book, you mentioned that you were on a 13-month service in Brunei. How did your time in Brunei changed how you see the world now?
Moments of solitude were plenty and like I said before, these moments yearn for reflections. The life there allows endless introspection through observances. Hardships and basic living were habitual. Not many choices were laid out either, so we were built to survive according to the environment to be forbearing.

Unknowingly, these moments strengthens the physical body and cleanses the soul - in which I mean the mind is granted clarity, the heart is instilled wisdom and the physical body is built.

So I came home a different man – a man with purpose.

7. What's your favourite verse/poem from your book and what inspired you to write it?
Unfortunately I don't have a favourite poem for I hold

each of them close to my heart. And every single one of them lies in it a unique memory, experience and lesson as a reminder for myself. To have a favourite would mean having one above the other, but I'd prefer to see it as everyone needed the other to make me who I am today.

8. Amidst all the chaos in the world, do you have something to say to other Muslim travellers who are unsure if they should travel at all?

Travel and trade were the main reasons how Islam expanded, and came to where we are today, so you realise how important it is to human/spiritual/intellectual development? Travel does not necessarily mean only going overseas, travelling from mosques to mosques, or mosque –hopping as people usually call it as an option too. However, do note that it is better not to travel if the reason and intention is twisted (example: to have nice Instagram photos to show off to others) for travelling is just a mean, enlightenment is the goal.

9. Do you have a favourite travel photo? If yes, why is it significant to you?

My favourite travel photo or photos would have to be the ones I took during my stint in Brunei. They held extremely unique and bittersweet memories that brought me to where

I am today. On a lighter note, I was at my best shape back then too!

10. Fill in the blank:

My hope for the world is… that we perfect our own moral character first and to leave what does not concern us.

About the Author

The Singaporean author, going by the pen name of The Vespa Rider is a writer, speaker, entrepreneur, certified hijama practitioner and an assistant engineer.

Prior to his writing endevours, he graduated from Ngee Ann Polytechnic with a Diploma in Marine & Offshore Technology before pursuing his Part-Time Diploma in Islamic Studies with International Islamic University of Malaysia (IIUM). He also earned his certification as Hijama practitioner from Hijama Associates.

The Vespa Rider has since written two poetry books, distributed worldwide. His first book Syafakallah May Allah swt Heal You, has won multiple awards such as 2016 Best-Selling Book of the Year and Top 10 Titles of All Time by well-renowned Wardah Books. His second book, La Taqlaq Do Not Worry was in the MPH Malaysia Top 10 Monthly Best-Seller. He is now in the works for his third. He was invited as speaker in mosques like Selangor International Islamic University College and other institutions such as Al-Qudwah Academy. He performed spoken word poetry for the Rohingya Conference – Digital ASEAN Migration & Youth Welfare in Kuala Lumpur and was also a judge for Youth of Darul Arqam (YODA) Spoken Word Competition.

His writings have appeared in magazines such as SUHUF by En-Naeem and has conducted writing workshops with Safinah Institute. He recently founded Bilal Books, a Muslim publishing and distribution platform based in Singapore. He hopes to empower budding writers to find their voice through words and to intrigue readers to translate words into change. One of his biggest dreams is to own a bookshop cum creative space and build a mosque that also serves as an orphanage and/or school.

He wishes to be reminded to be nothing but a contented struggling soul. Someone who seeks to observe life to its detailed wisdoms while remembering the certainty of death in the uncertainty of time.

*"The goal isn't to appeal to the masses,
the goal is to awaken."*
- Dulce Ruby

E-mail:
iamthevesparider@gmail.com

Instagram:
@iamthevesparider
@thevesparider.books

Twitter:
@TheVespaRider

Hashtag:
#nowreadingsyafakallah

About Bilal Books

Bilal Books (UEN: 53392752L) launched in 2019 as a Muslim publishing and distribution platform based in Singapore.

To be a medium of assistance and motivation to readers and writers alike, empowering writers to find their voice through words and intriguing readers to translate words into change.

Other published books by Bilal Books:

La Taqlaq (Do Not Worry) by The Vespa Rider
Healing Carefulliy by Nurliyana Rahmat
-

Official Website:
www.bilalbooks.com

E-mail:
books@bilalbooks.com

Instagram:
@bilal.books

Hashtag:
#nowreadinglataqlaq
#healingcarefulliy

Stockist & Distributorship

Worldwide Distributor:

www.bilalbooks.com

Singapore

Wardah Books
58 Bussorah St, Singapore 199474

Salaam Media International
#01-40/74, Golden Landmark Shopping Centre,
390 Victoria Street, Singapore 188061

English Islamic Bookshop
Darul Arqam, 32 Onan Rd, Singapore 424484

Muslimedia Bookshop
448 Changi Road, #01-05 Singapore 419975

Malaysia

Iman Shoppe
8, Jalan Dagang SB 4/2, Taman Sungai Besi Indah,
43300 Seri Kembangan,
Selangor, Malaysia

Dakwah Corner Bookstore
No. 7, Jalan Dato Abdul Aziz 14/29, Section 14, 46100
Petaling Jaya, Selangor D.E

<u>Nur Innai Bookshop</u>
C-0-5, Jalan Sri Hartamas, Taman Sri Hartamas, 50480
Kuala Lumpur, Wilayah Persekutuan Kuala Lumpur

<u>Bookstore Chains</u>
Kinokuniya, MPH Bookstores, BORDERS, Popular,
Gallery Bookstore & SMO Bookstores

Brunei

<u>Nolly Book</u>
Unit R4, Departure Hall Brunei International Airport,
Muara, Brunei

<u>DBookHaus</u>
1.23A, First Floor, The Mall, Gadong,
Bandar Seri Begawan, Brunei

<u>The Story Shop</u>
Ground Floor, No. 6, Kiulap, Bandar Seri Begawan, Brunei

Philippines

<u>Topreads MyChoiceofBooks</u>
Marawi and Iligan City
IG: @topreadsph

<u>Iqra The Book Corner</u>
9700 Marawi City, MSU Main Campus
IG: @iqrathebookcorner

Australia

<u>Sakeena Books</u>
www.sakeenabooks.com